The Power

Of

Self confidence

Ways to boost your self-confidence effectively

By

EDEN WILSON

To my readers, and listeners.

To a lot of people reading this book
I know for a fact that I would not have had
the confidence
to write this book, if it wasn't for your
support.

Therefore I humbly dedicate it to
each and every one of you.

Table of contents

Introduction

Your thoughts, reflections, and even random ones may help you become more confident, but to really benefit from them, you must be conscious of them.

Study has shown that the human brain is capable of thought. It might be a combination of five to nine things happening at once. It might be difficult to separate the ideas that boost your confidence from those that are harmful. Being conscious of your inner confidence is the first step, even if it has been hidden for some time. The second one is to concentrate on your self-assurance. It's hard to be confident. I advise you to do it if you find some quiet time for introspection while feeling this way to help you recognize the self-assurance you possess when you have positive self and life esteem. We all know that if you've done something before, you can do it again, therefore they are confident recollections. Because you aren't simply wishing and hoping, but really realizing that you have been (and can be) a more confident person, reflecting on prior triumphs and allowing yourself to experience the good feelings associated with them can help you establish a better capacity to tap into your confidence.

Those little bits of achievement, pride, and certainty are like seeds: If you plant them, give them a little water and sunshine (or in this instance, some time and thinking), they will grow and you will start to feel better about yourself and what you are doing. This activity provides a workout for your emotions, even if it doesn't entail lifting weights or donning shoes. Most individuals are first a little hesitant, in part because they are entering new terrain, which always causes a little bit of worry. You'll be happy you took on the effort of overcoming your uneasiness and genuinely working to determine where your confidence rests after you've finished it.

Your life will become a little bit simpler and perhaps a lot more enjoyable once you realize that you have the capacity to believe in oneself (since you have experienced it previously). Instead of trying to rule the world, being confident is making the most of your surroundings. Take some time to seek it; it doesn't take much, and you do have it inside your heart and soul. What you discover should make you feel quite good about yourself.

Rebuild your confidence

There are several simple things you may take to rebuild your confidence when things spiral out of hand and you suddenly lose it. Here are 10 resources to get you going.

1. Brush your teeth and wash your hands and face. It provides you that "new start" sense by cooling your body, which is calming.

2. Take a look at any awards you may have, such as diplomas or certificates. And put it up on the wall if it isn't already framed. These serve as reminders of your successes, and acknowledging your achievements is crucial to preserving your confidence.

3. Think of your most recent or best achievement for 60 seconds. You may

achieve one achievement after another by savoring it as frequently as you can. Simply put, it serves as a reminder that you can succeed again because you have done it before.

4. Shave your head well (face or legs). Another quick refreshment, plus the fact that we feel more confidence when we know we are looking our best.

5. Recognize that you are who your children or other loved ones believe you to be. You can't help but feel good about yourself when you realize that you are loved unconditionally.

6. Inside and out, wash your vehicle. Hey, we feel better when our wheels are shining. If you don't believe this applies to you, think back to the last time you were taken

somewhere in a particularly unusual vehicle. Go to the vehicle wash before you.

7. Put on fresh socks and shoes that you haven't worn in a couple of days. This is a fairly simple approach to add a little spring to your step. Shoes need a day or two to discharge whatever moisture they have absorbed.

8. Sort through your wardrobe and get rid of everything that doesn't fit. Even while worn-out clothing may come back into fashion, you shouldn't leave it hanging for another 10 years. Making place for the new by getting rid of the old. Some people feel more confident after donning a new "power suit" because of the way it makes them feel.

9. Make a delicious supper. Even if you are dining alone, making a delicious meal, setting the table, and rewarding yourself

with a memorable meal can make you feel
better. It will become much more nurturing
if you share it with someone you love and/or
respect.

10. Take a look about you and realize that
everything you see is something you
produced. Especially when something goes
wrong in our life, we might all lose our sense
of self-worth. The fact is that you can
accomplish anything after you've done it
before. Whatever the case,

You won't spend much time on any of these
duties, and none of them need to be
unpleasant. Truly confident individuals
often use the technique of finding methods
to give themselves a tiny boost when they
don't feel at their best.

The impact of Negativity on your confidence

Toxic surroundings include those where individuals are rude or even aggressive to one another. Nobody attempts to make you or anybody else feel better, and nobody can find emotional or even physical consolation. This will make you feel less valuable and may even make you lose the desire to live.Having the odd poor day or moment is not the point of this. Living and/or working in a setting that degrades you is the subject. If you hang around for a long time and someone keeps telling you that you're not good enough, ultimately you'll start to believe it. Only two animals on the planet

dogs and people will accept it and believe it
if you repeatedly tell them they are awful.

 All of us have seen pets whose spirits were
crushed. They go about with their heads
down and their tails tucked between their
legs. They respond fearfully and aggressively
when shocked or afraid (barking or growling
when they are frightened). The unfortunate
creatures never seem to feel secure. It's
terrible to see that they have lost their wag.
When someone puts them down often at
home or when they work for an organization
that uses intimidation to run things, people
often respond in similar ways. There isn't
much pleasure to be had here, and one's
self-confidence might quickly be destroyed.
The majority of individuals in such
situations just don't have the energy to find

the strength they need to fight the forces that are assaulting them.

The key is to take a step back far enough to get perspective. If the situation I just described really exists, therapy hasn't helped, or has been rejected, the wisest course of action could be to just leave. I realize that's extreme, but "battered person's syndrome" is a term used to describe remaining in a bad situation or relationship out of fear of moving on, such as when abused women return to their abusers' homes. They do it, foolishly believing that the devil they know is superior to the one they don't. They're going back to a place they know.

Keep going

For the next day, you had a fantastic plan. Even though you went to bed early in hopes of waking up with a little extra energy to work on your current project, something unexpected occurred. An issue that you had not foreseen happened after being agitated knocked you unconscious somewhere during the night or possibly after receiving a phone call or nudge in the early morning. Your well-laid plans have failed miserably. We typically experience a little amount of anxiety and even complete panic when the unexpected occurs. Again, this is very typical behavior for individuals, but the issue is that when this happens, confidence is often shattered, which makes it harder for people to alter course (or just get lost) and get back on track.

Here is an alternative strategy to maintain your concentration and advance the procedure: Take the time to complete your job as planned rather than putting it on hold to address the issue that is attempting to attract your attention. You maintain control by resisting the urge to veer off course. Despite your present (and most likely temporary) circumstances, if you can sit down and finish your objective, you won't lose any ground and will boost your self-confidence.

Knowing that you can avoid mental musings and excuses no matter what occurs allows you to concentrate when under stress and complete the task at hand. Making the necessary progress despite short-term failures will make you feel good about yourself.

Additionally, since you won't be worried about what you haven't accomplished, you will be better able to concentrate on the issue that disturbed you. Along with getting greater clarity, you could even come up with some new solutions on how to solve your problem while doing the task at hand. Use your unconscious mind whenever you can to develop your problem-solving abilities. We've all had the experience of having better ideas when our thoughts aren't focused on the issue we're attempting to address.

You could also be able to direct your anxiety into something considerably more constructive. Nobody benefits from you just being frantic and neglecting what you had intended to accomplish. However, if others around you see your ability to complete tasks despite the fact that everything is going to hell in a handbasket, everyone will have a greater sense of confidence in you.

Putting out flames might sometimes be a technique to put off doing what is really necessary. So before you put your priorities on hold, be sure the emergency is genuine and you are indeed required. The fact is that you are capable of doing your assignment and saving the planet.

Be Patient

Don't consider it a failure if you don't achieve your objectives the first time you attempt. Keep in mind that you have gained knowledge and will do better the following time. Knowing that you will learn from every event, no matter what, is the key to developing self-confidence.

It is simple to become irritated and angry, but imagine how different life would be if Thomas Edison had given up on his quest to create the electric light after many failures. He has the patience to carry out all of his many ideas.

Self-assurance doesn't come from waiting around impatiently for things to happen. It involves hurling everything against the wall and patiently waiting for anything to stick. The next step is to carefully craft your projects. That is often the most challenging step in the procedure. When it comes to putting their ideas into action, great innovators may sometimes be quite impatient.

Keep in mind that no one can stand up for you while you are being impatient with yourself. We need to go from "deadlines" we set for ourselves to "preferred time lines." Unconsciously, missing a deadline makes you anxious because you subconsciously believe that you will die if the task is not completed. That also occurs when someone doesn't provide you with what you believe you need at the time that you believe you need it. Your subconscious is really warning you that you could lose something extremely significant to you, which may make you feel anxious. Getting anything done is more difficult when you're under that kind of stress.

Realizing how you respond to those close to you might help you practice patience by making yourself take your time. Being irritated with them indicates a lack of self-confidence since it's possible that you'll be irritable with yourself as well. By putting more effort into going with the flow, you may learn to be more patient with yourself when life gets in the way or takes more time than you anticipated. Simply reminding yourself that Rome wasn't built in a day and that whatever you are engaged in is worth the time you are spending may help you maintain your composure if you start to feel impatient.

Although patience is a virtue, it is also essential to obtaining and leading a life of self-assurance.

Be prepared

If you don't know what you need to know, you can't be confident. Learn, do your homework, and never stop reading. Whether you're preparing for a presentation or a date, doing so will make you feel more secure and enable you to showcase your finest qualities.

Making sure everything is in order also makes it easier to prepare for the unexpected. You may not have brought every technique in the book with you, but you have undoubtedly read about them. The inevitable inquiry you were scared to ask becomes simple to answer if you are prepared.

No, you can't always be prepared for anything life brings your way. But once you develop the habit of planning, you accumulate emotional building blocks that you may draw upon later. Please believe me on this one; there is no work wasted. Even if you don't utilize what you're planning for right now tomorrow, you will in the future.

Emotional preparation is just as crucial as mental and physical preparation. The most effective strategy, in my experience, is to mentally picture what you are going to perform. If you're taking an exam, see yourself succeeding. When making a speech, see the crowd nodding in agreement and cheering (maybe even giggling at your jokes). I'm convinced this method, which is used to treat cancer, will boost your confidence. Additionally, it will assist you in finishing the work at hand.

You must have studied or be able to study to be mentally prepared. Men are said to never bother reading manuals; although this may have been true before the advent of technology, it is not true now. Before trying to connect your new video-game system, at the very least, read the instructions since life is just too hard to do otherwise.

Making a mental or written checklist before starting a project, whether it be new or old, is a practical step that can only increase your feeling of confidence. Additionally, it will make you consider items you may have overlooked, and you won't be left wondering what to do with the spare components.

When you are doing something as straightforward as going to the market, creating a checklist could seem a bit over the top if you are simply going out for dinner and a movie. Without to-do lists, I don't know how anybody would survive. They could be the one thing that helps us the most get things done and remain on schedule.

Another excellent method of preparedness is, if necessary, to take safety measures: As you prepare to climb the Matterhorn in the Alps, you meticulously arrange your equipment and mentally rehearse utilizing it. By lowering your anxiety while you tee up your ball and check your surroundings to ensure that you won't accidentally hit your

boss with your Big Bertha driver, you are
also getting ready to hit a superb shot.
Your pal and it's not nearly as painful as you
think it is, preparation. Additionally, it is
essential for boosting self-assurance.

Recognition is more than money

You also live a better life when you have a sphere of influence and provide a platform for others to develop their own confidence. We do it to create the future and fill our own lives.

Everyone carries baggage with them that prevents them from becoming their best selves. Check the bags for them as part of your duty (or at least make sure they are carry-on). Because he will realize that he is not struggling alone, it will encourage him to be his best self. He will have a lot more positive feelings about you, your talk, and your relationship with him.

Saying "Thanks" may go a long way toward improving someone's self-esteem. You'd be astonished at how many individuals believe that their lives are lived in anonymity. You may motivate someone without expending a lot of time and effort by giving them a pat on the back, a handwritten message of gratitude, or a tiny symbol of appreciation.

When was the last time you just expressed gratitude to your loved ones for being there in your life? Have you acknowledged the persons you collaborate with and who assist you in making that aspect of your life as simple as possible? And then there are individuals that we seldom ever see or, in the digital era, never see at all. How can you express your gratitude for their involvement in your world? When applicable, I make care

to include personal messages and
thoroughly thank them for their assistance.

The majority of people seem happy with the
acknowledgment, and I feel good about
myself for considering doing it and really
doing it. Your interpersonal and
professional connections will only benefit
from it. Giving confidence via appreciation
has numerous positive side effects.
It will promote good in every manner,
shape, and form to assist individuals in
improving their self-esteem. Test it out.

Embrace your fears

It seems to be the reason that facing your fears would make you stronger and more independent. You may overcome your anxieties in a far more effective and useful manner by accepting them. To overcome your worries, you don't necessarily need to scale Mount Everest or leap out of a perfectly excellent aircraft; often, simply knowing how to handle the stress and concern of regular life will boost your confidence.

A successful medical friend of mine says he feels afraid every day, but he embraces it because he really thinks it makes him a better doctor. He is more cautious and doesn't endanger his patients needlessly. It motivates him to perform at the highest level and cultivates his confidence as a practitioner.

I once heard that faith is the antithesis of fear, and although I can see how having confidence in a higher force may give you a sense of security, I also believe that knowing the source of your worries and learning the lessons they can impart on us are extremely powerful weapons.
There is usually a benefit to our worries. Yes, they may protect us physically from falling off a cliff or trying to touch a tiger, but there is much more to our phobias than just keeping us safe. Fears may help us become more self-aware and recognize where we need to make changes in order to

have the strength to complete the job at hand. An excellent activity to help you not only conquer your fears but also utilize them to achieve your objectives is to have the courage to wrap your mind around them and consider how they assist or damage you. It will be challenging to become a leader, public personality, or movie star if you get panic attacks at the mere prospect of speaking in front of a large group of people. You may, however, become aware of your (obvious) shortcomings.

Along with gaining the resources you need for success, you will develop a talent that will enable you to realize your goals and boost your confidence as you go. It is possible to let go of whatever pretense you may have had and feel good about improving at public speaking once you acknowledge to yourself that you suffer from what is considered to be the most common fear in the world: public speaking.

Nobody I know who has faced and conquered their anxieties hasn't benefited from it and become more self-assured. With the understanding that you will defeat the mental demons by facing whatever it is that terrifies you to death, you should attack it.

Find a Mentor

It's not too late if your parents didn't raise you in a way that gave you the confidence you now possess. Find a mentor in a subject that you are passionate about and someone you respect. Most individuals will do their best to assist you since they are touched by your request.

Life coaching or even therapy are not what mentoring is. It is a method by which someone who is eager to impart her expertise and experience and who is more knowledgeable and experienced than you in certain areas helps you negotiate the choppy waters of business and life.

After you've discovered each other, the first thing to do is to talk about and settle on the nature and objectives of your partnership. Take your time with this chat since it will set the tone for your future activities together. In many facets of your life, you may have mentors. An effective mentor may be worth their weight in gold. The ups and downs that come with sharing your life with another person may be managed with the aid of your relationship mentor. It's also possible to have a mentor for sports like tennis or fishing, which differs from taking lessons since the mentor is concerned with your total wellbeing rather than simply showing you how to "become better at it."

For instance, I mentor and play what I have come to refer to as Zen tennis rather than competitive tennis. In order to keep the volley running as long as possible, you must strike the ball in such a manner that your partner (not your opponent) can easily return it. Not only winning is the goal; playing is as well. It's a fantastic method to work out while honing your aim and purpose on the court. In addition, nobody feels defeated since it's enjoyable, useful exercise, and everyone wins. Having a mentor may be helpful in any aspect of your life and is a terrific confidence booster.

Relationships between mentors and mentees almost never don't turn out well. Everyone outgrows their mentor at some point, and the relationship changes to something different, yet the connection that was made will always exist (unless you want it to). The good news is that if you have a situation that you'd want to run by your mentor, you can always pick up the phone and call him.

The confidence you get from being close to someone you can trust, who is knowledgeable in her field and is aware of who you are, is a priceless gift. It's not too late to find a mentor if you've never had one. The issues we confront in the modern world are not going away; rather, they are just becoming more complex, so if it has been a while, obtaining another one would be a smart idea.

Our confidence is shaken when we are in a state of bewilderment and are unsure of what to do. Speaking with a mentor is a

terrific method to boost your confidence,
remind you that you are clever and skilled,
and provide you with someone to assist you
overcome the difficulties in life and in love.

The power of clarity towards confidence

It is really powerful to know that you are correct and to feel this way inside of oneself. You must learn to trust your instincts and check in with your thoughts and emotions to remove any obstacles that could be in the way of getting there.

Asking yourself "clarifying questions" is the first step you should do if you are having difficulty. Imagine someone is attempting to assist you and will need some clarity on what the problem is. This will enable you to know what questions to ask. Now pose those same questions to yourself. It may be beneficial to jot down both your queries and responses.

Consider the issue from all potential angles. It might be helpful to run the issue past a trusted individual to get his opinion. He could ask you further questions and assist you in gaining greater clarity. Once you are aware of the true problems, you may start to develop solutions.

Questions like "how much?" "how long?" and "why are we doing this?" may all be used as clarifications.

Don't restrict yourself; this exercise costs you nothing and will provide you with the knowledge you need to make a conclusion that you are confident in.

Saving time and money by developing your
ability to ask the correct questions of
yourself can also make you feel more in
control of your life.

Be open to new ideas

True learning revolves on being open to new
concepts while attempting to solve an issue.
Believe in your own abilities and the
abilities of others you may trust.
It will be difficult to advance or simply
survive where you are if you attempt to
handle everything on your own,
micro-manage every aspect, and reject fresh
ideas from people around you.

It is usually a good idea to get advice from
the knowledgeable individuals you have
surrounded yourself with. You're going to be
impacted by everything and everyone
around you unless you choose to live in a
remote hut with no access to the outside

world. Accept the influence, let it ingrain itself in you, and let it mold you into the finest version of yourself.

Just remember to pay due respect to those who served as your inspiration.

It makes sense: Telling someone she had a wonderful suggestion that you'd want to implement would be seen as a compliment if you're confident in yourself. And the reality is that their suggestion did, in fact, enhance yours.

The "out there" idea, the one you were simply joking around with, may sometimes have the most effect. When you do it with other people, you may refer to it as brainstorming, but I refer to it as playing with ideas.

Sometimes remarks made only for laughs or to elicit an emotional response (kids are amazing at this) turn out to be concepts that completely hit home with you.

When you are being severe on yourself or your confidence is low, you could choose to dismiss the solutions or suggestions that sometimes pop into your thoughts. We all confront the task of learning to be receptive to our own ideas, particularly in trying circumstances.

Your experience and level of confidence will be severely constrained if you are not receptive to multiple forms of intelligence (ideas from the world around you and learning through experience).

Build a Strong Foundation

A solid foundation gives you the knowledge, power, and self-assurance you need to build anything you want and travel anywhere you want.

Those who have realized their aspirations are aware of this fundamental reality.

There is nothing wrong with studying, relearning, or practicing to strengthen your foundation even if you don't currently have all you need. Self-assured individuals take the required actions to get the knowledge and assistance they need since they are aware of their ignorance and are at ease understanding it.

It might be easier to understand the value of a solid foundation if you consider how your life is constructed similarly to how a home is constructed. Choosing the kind of foundation you want and require is the first step in building a house. Similar choices must be made if you are launching a new firm. You must do your research and ensure that your team includes the correct bankers, brokers, and business advisors. Everything comes together if the team and structure are in place, giving your house, company, or new life a solid launchpad.

All individuals, houses, and companies need routine maintenance, and maybe even significant repairs along the road. These things don't indicate failure; they just happen over time. The majority of professionals will advise you that if your home has a solid foundation and healthy bones, you may make whatever repairs you need, as well as remodel or expand. This holds true for the remainder of your life.

You won't get out of your situation by being harsh with yourself because things didn't go as planned (welcome to the human race). Dealing with any unanticipated challenge is made much simpler by relying on the basis of what you know you can do. You can overcome any problem that arises right now if you have the necessary resources, such as self-assurance in your abilities or access to a killer team and support system.

You may build the life, career, or house that you want without a formal education by using your skills, experiences, and other people's strengths as your foundation. Our pillars may be found everywhere. Maybe your dad taught you how to build and mend things, or maybe your mom gave you a knack for decorating and a drive to do it, and you've always been excellent at it without really understanding why. Because you have a solid foundation whether it's inherited, natural, or learned, respecting it is the first step toward developing more self-confidence.

Depend on yourself

You have the resources you need to go through a difficult time or start something new and amazing in your life when you know you can depend on the people you love, the people on your team, and maybe most significantly, yourself.

It's not impossible to try to accomplish it alone in the world today, but it will take a very, very long time. Your life will be simpler if you have someone to rely on, and you will get the confidence that comes from understanding that you don't have to accomplish everything on your own. Taking pleasure in your dependability will only make you more self-assured and

dependable since you like the positive vibe it
brings. It makes its way into your brain and
encourages you to feel good about yourself,
the project you are working on, and the
individuals you are supporting or helping.
Everything turns into a force for good. There
is an esprit de corps that arises when a
group of individuals work effectively
together on a project, and you all get to
enjoy the positive energy.
Being the reliable one isn't dull; rather, it
will eventually increase your attractiveness.
We become weary of being disappointed or
dealing with flakes as we get older.

If others feel they can rely on you, you may
find real love or go up the corporate ladder.
There isn't a river you can't bridge or an
issue you can't solve when you genuinely

understand that you can rely on yourself. Knowing that you or the other person you need will be there will give you confidence, period.

Differentiate between your needs and wants

Without our moms, particularly the mother of innovation, where would we be? One of the finest ways to establish your essential status is to identify a need and meet it.

Being required is one of life's best motivators and confidence boosters, as well. It will be almost hard for you to avoid feeling a bit better about yourself in the process if you have the strength to give of yourself when it is required. This will only help to increase the confidence that people have in you.

Making the right judgments requires having the ability to distinguish between what you need and what you desire. Understanding the distinction between appetite and hunger is one of the simplest ways to approach the issue. Your stomach signals to your brain, "Feed me," when you are hungry because your body needs food since it is short on calories and energy.

However, appetite is the desire for food that looks or smells good. Although you may not even be hungry, you yearn for the delectable aromas and salivate at the thought of the upcoming taste. Let's look at how it pertains to how you see your personal requirements vs wants now that you have a basic knowledge of the difference. Start by doing a "necessity triage," which will assist you in determining what constitutes a need before placing your needs in the proper context. Be really honest with yourself when you make a list of the items you believe you need. Are they really necessities or are they only wants? You will probably discover that a lot of what you first thought you required is really a wish, and that you already have 99 percent of what you need. That alone is a fantastic confidence booster. Additionally, being certain that your needs are met will free you up to give of yourself since you will be confident in your ability to do so on a physical, emotional, and financial level.

Additionally, keep in mind that labor is the mother of innovation, so be ready to work toward your goals.

Be courageous

Courage is not the absence of fear; rather, it is the ability to push through uncertain circumstances in order to accomplish your objectives. A foundational element of confidence is taking on tasks with the knowledge that you have the emotional fortitude to face the trials that lie ahead. Many problems, both personal and professional, may be overcome with awareness of your surroundings and the knowledge that you are on the correct road. Consider it a journey (or your commute if you reside in Los Angeles): How far ahead do you glance while driving on the freeway? You probably won't notice the collision that happened half a mile ahead and all the vehicles in front of you slamming on their brakes if it's just at the car directly in front of you. If you had looked that half a mile ahead, you would have noticed the collision in plenty of time to prevent hitting someone in the back.

People that have courage are aware of their surroundings. They are generally equipped both inwardly and externally to cope with changes and problems because they can feel when things change. The courageous seem to be used to handling tense circumstances, but in reality, most just have faith that they are acting morally, and if they find themselves in an unforeseen position, they improvise by making do with what they have at hand. The capacity to keep an eye on their surroundings and have enough composure to handle whatever comes their way is what gives courageous individuals their confidence. It's possible that they are more resourceful than bold, but whatever the case, their confidence depends on it.

Knowing that you are doing morally gives you a sense of power. And having that level of assurance will inevitably give you the guts you need to overcome obstacles. You have a far better chance of succeeding if you believe that you are destined to be where you are or to withstand whatever hazard you are facing, whether it be a health condition, a career obstacle, or a relationship problem.

There are various sources of courage, and it is confidence that allows you to withstand an intimidating situation. The majority of individuals experience anxiety while trying a new sport, going on a first date, or enrolling in a new class. Nobody wants to seem unattractive to their onlooker friends, a prospective love interest, or a group of curious onlookers. Knowing that we all experience the same things should give you courage to take on anything new or somewhat threatening.

The fact is that you've gone this far, gained a lot of knowledge, endured some tragedies, and had your mettle put to the test in a variety of ways.
That ought to offer you the assurance that you won't only survive the unfamiliar but also find the bravery to do some things that may be further outside of your comfort zone than they may have been in the past.

Don't isolation yourself

There have been studies for many years showing that persons who live with others live longer than those who live alone. Additionally, more recent studies have found that living alone could be worse for your physical health than smoking. This doesn't imply that you will pass away too soon if you are content in your single status, but it should cause you to reconsider life and love in a new way.

We're not supposed to live alone. There are a couple billion individuals in the world, which alone is proof of that. Nevertheless, millions of people who have been harmed or traumatized by a fellow human would want to stay away from other Homo sapiens.

Those who have survived relationships with a lot of turmoil may find it simpler to focus on taking care of themselves, as well as potentially their kids or pets. It may be draining to deal with the vagaries of another person, particularly if that person is also being difficult toward you.
To keep your independence and sanity while having a close connection with another adult, you will need to be creative and find some of the numerous ways to share your life and your bed with someone but still needing your privacy.

Many non-living-together couples have "nights off"; they have created safe boundaries that enable them to enjoy their own time without making their spouse feel anxious. Typically, keeping in touch just requires a brief phone contact before the night off, followed by a catch-up discussion ("Did you sleep well?").

Have a serious discussion about the behavior and determine the reason if the person you love often withdraws and you have to go looking for them. The depth of your love will be diminished if you feel abandoned as a result of this sort of behavior.

You are also harming yourself if you isolate as a tactic of retaliation. Even though this passive-aggressive approach may seem appropriate at the time, you will eventually feel lonely since you never said what it was that first harmed you. And if you don't express what irritates you, it won't go away. People who isolate themselves may be struggling with despair and/or anxiety; they have the delusion that being alone would make everything better. Even though not everyone who likes to be alone suffers from a mood condition, you should see a doctor if you're feeling down.

The sensation of safety or empowerment that comes from being cut off from the rest of humanity is fleeting. Furthermore, it is difficult to feel secure when there is no one around to affirm your presence. We are social creatures, so having someone to share life with makes it much more meaningful.

Live a good life

At the conclusion of Saving Private Ryan, an elderly soldier who has been rescued sobs as he asks his wife whether he has had a happy life. Self-worth and genuine pleasure are rooted in the knowledge that we have made the world a little bit better than when we discovered it. not the type you get from visiting Disneyworld, but rather from knowing deep down that you've changed something.

Do not undervalue it. The ability to contribute and be a part of something that strengthens society at large or your local community may be very therapeutic for all parties concerned. It helps you develop your internal 401k and leads to greater relationships and better emotional wellness. Even while you may not really generate any money, you are investing in your value, and that often yields greater returns.

Being Volunteer of the Year and giving up necessities or things you enjoy are not requirements for living a fulfilling life. It implies that you pay attention to your inner guidance when it suggests that you may assist someone in need. Most of us can't just up and go to Africa to help with relief operations, but I believe we can all do something little to help others who are less fortunate (versus a handout). You may not be able to provide money right now, but you can contribute your ideas, emotional support, and even your own email list.

Finding methods to include others is also a smart use of your time, and it can be the just the justification you need to get in touch with some past acquaintances.

I have a small list of folks I contact when a worthwhile cause hits my heart to ask for help (typically a contribution), so that I may have a somewhat bigger influence. Contrary to popular belief, these people truly appreciate the calls. Like many of us, they want to contribute to the solution since it feels good to know that you have changed something.

Giving to others improves our feeling of self. It produces brain chemicals that actually increase our capacity for happiness and lower our levels of worry and despair. I've seen many cynics rejoice at the thought that they gave someone hope who they would never see again. Even the simplest act of kindness from a complete stranger may make a world of difference when you are suffering or just feeling depressed. You are aware if you have ever been there.

Living a good life is about contributing in a manner that will mean something to you, not about how much you give. It does not need to be material or monetary. Sometimes a nice word and a reaching hand are the most priceless gifts you can give.

The powers of positive thinking

When people begin to believe they can do things, they start to become really very exceptional. The first key to success is having confidence in oneself.

We all sometimes think and speak negatively about ourselves. It's quite typical. Unfortunately, if you have a tendency of thinking in this manner, it might prevent you from enjoying life, achieving your objectives, or even falling in love.

Being conscious of the negative thoughts as they occur is one technique to overcome this habit. This kind of awareness might make

the event more enjoyable. Real stress
reduction comes from being aware of what
is happening both within your thoughts and
in your life.

Try taking a tablet for patience if you are
aware that you are stressed out. Tell yourself
to accept the situation as it is until the
uncomfortable or unpleasant thoughts or
moments pass. We often think negatively
when we don't feel good about ourselves.
Maybe your boyfriend, parents, or employer
criticized you or broke a commitment to
you, making you feel depressed. This might
be hard to avoid occasionally in real life.

However, being conscious of how you are
really feeling at the time allows you to alter
the energy and defend yourself by
deliberately thinking good ideas. Being

optimistic is not the same as being this. A tried-and-true method that can help you change your mood is to use your own thinking to help you solve a problem.
It also helps to be grateful for where you are and what you have. Additionally, you must promise yourself that you won't allow upsetting feelings or circumstances control your life or draw you in. Utilize the power of positive thought to prevent a terrible situation from becoming a way of life.

Here are some helpful pointers to get you going:
• List the things in your life that are effective in your mind. This sets the tone for getting through a challenging situation. Then, to get more internal support, consider how you've handled similar situations in the past.

• Do you still remember "The Little Engine That Could"?

Declare, "I believe I can," to yourself. It could be more effective to say, "I know I can."

• Stop the negative idea when you hear yourself saying, "I'm not good enough," and instead say, "I'm canceling that out." Replace that with a confident remark, such as "I've succeeded before and I can do it again."

Positive ideas offer you more energy than negative ones do, so that's another incentive to place a plus sign in your mental minus column. You just need to perform the arithmetic to know that the effort is worthwhile.

Negative thinking may really hurt you and your loved ones, particularly if you (or they) start to believe it. It's not simply a poor habit. So stop listening to the depressing station in your thoughts and start focusing on the positive things you do and have. It will make your world a better place.

Avoid procrastination

I've been meaning to do this for a long time, but it's so simple to come up with something better to do. That is the procrastinator's guiding principle. Do not misunderstand me; I really think that nothing would be done if it weren't for the final minute. But if you are causing yourself misery because you lack the motivation to complete what has to be done, it's time to break that habit. To assist you in doing that, read the following advice.

All depends on timing. Measure the time it takes you to complete some of the tasks you put off. For instance, the guy in my mirror despises cleaning the dishes. I used to let them accumulate in the sink. Then, one day, in a rush, I happened to look at the time just as I started rinsing my hands in soapy water.

When I was done, I checked the time again and saw that only six minutes had elapsed. I can do the task much more quickly now that I know it won't take as long as all the things I tried to avoid. And home life is a little more enjoyable.

Just do it. Many Olympic-level procrastinators waste their time looking for shortcuts or using avoidance strategies like declaring, "That's not my job," or wondering, "Who else can I get to do this?" In actuality, if you just get started on the work at hand, you will have some additional time in your life, which you may utilize anyway you choose.

Get over your fear. It can't feel nice to avoid something because the notion of having to do it or failing at it makes you anxious. You are basically making an excuse to put off or ignore key aspects of your life in addition to overcoming the fear component. It will be beneficial to ask your spouse or a friend to help you with a task if you are afraid of it. Simply being in someone's presence may be a powerful incentive for many. Working over your fear can make you and your relationships stronger. Fear may hold us back from many things in life.

Make time for resting. We put off doing the things we need to accomplish a lot because we are simply plain exhausted.
One of the greatest methods to deal with this is to treat yourself to a sleep or some relaxation once you've finished what has to be done. No one of us can be productive constantly, and having a good night's sleep really sharpens your mind, so taking a break is necessary.

While overcoming procrastination is a positive thing, you shouldn't punish yourself while doing so. This habit was not developed overnight by you, and just reflecting on it won't make it go away. One step at a time, make progress in your life, and before you realize it, you'll appreciate your life and your productivity much more.

Train your mind

Everyone who has achieved success in their chosen area, gotten promoted, or won a game has put in many hours of practice—both physically and mentally.

As there are things to practice for, there are also several methods to do so. Even if you don't believe you have the time to practice, there is always a good moment. The benefit of mental rehearsal is that you may do it while eating breakfast or traveling to an event, which is also highly beneficial. What works for you may not work for someone else, but everyone who wants to become better at anything in their life has to practice on a regular basis.

Additionally, there is practice while doing. You practice simply by doing what you want to grow great at. You may take on the next assignment and the one after that with the confidence you get from each advancement. Every time, you can be practicing for something a little bit different, perhaps something bigger and more difficult. You will continue to benefit from the confidence you develop as a result of all your hard work. The reward is when you discover how effectively you have practiced—for example, when you can deliver a speech at the drop of a hat.

Wouldn't it be wonderful to possess that level of assurance? The fact is that individuals who practice regularly have the self-assurance to jump in when the chance presents itself.

I place a lot of importance on mental practice. It is a frequent activity for astronauts and Olympians.

The majority of accomplished artists and entertainers also practice mentally. Some refer to it as visualization, while others use the term therapeutic guided imagery. Whatever it is called, people who employ some kind of mental rehearsal to hone their skills have the best chance of succeeding.

Your ability to compete at the greatest level is a result of your mix of mental, physical, and emotional practice. Try it out.

Level up your support structure

Before psychotherapy ever existed, there were support groups. The women of the ancient tribes cared for one another and the children and were permitted to seek advice from the chief when necessary. Medicine men would meet together and exchange their newest instruments. Join a group or start your own if your friends, family, or workplace aren't there to support you emotionally.

The latter may actually be simpler in this situation than the former since organizations that already exist want you to conform to their worldview, which might completely turn off certain individuals. Additionally, it could be challenging to locate a group that fully meets your requirements; thus, forming your own, even informally, can greatly benefit you in both life and company.

In Emotional Fitness at Work, I wrote about the advantages and magic of mastermind groups. These high-level meetings are for those who know they are excellent but desire to attain greatness; they are not for folks who require a 12-step program. Leaders and people just starting out in their professions may both benefit from peer learning. Most people discover that they don't need to reinvent the wheel since the other group members may have dealt with

the same challenges, and their knowledge
and counsel is invaluable.
Aside from information, organizations also
provide emotional support. Anyone who has
been there may relate to the proverb "It's
lonely at the top."
Although it's crucial to express your
emotions, a leader can't just go sobbing on
their vice president's shoulder and expect to
keep their respect. We all experience
overload, so having a space to let off steam
or just vent is something we all need to do
sometimes.

It is so much simpler when there is a secure
location to accomplish this.
However, you may want to incorporate
business and emotions into your chat, so
you must locate a counselor or group that

shares your goals. This is again not a simple
task, so let's look at how to put your own
together. Group or even individual
counseling is also highly beneficial.
Since he was a young child, my buddy Brad
Oberwager, the CEO of Sundria
Corporation, has known about and/or
participated in a support group for CEOs.
His father was a member of the Young
Presidents Organization (YPO), and by
sharing that experience with students at the
Wharton Business School, he founded a club
that still meets often today. He belongs to
the Young Entrepreneurs Organization as
well.

He attributes some of his success to these
organizations, and even in a bad economy,
his company is expanding. He gets the best

of both worlds and learns things that couldn't be learned from 20 years of graduate school by starting his own organization and joining one that has been active for a few decades.

So get out your old phone books, take a look at the individuals you get along with, and start dialing those whose expertise you wish to gain. Most likely, they'll think the concept is good and come to your meeting; from there, you can all decide if you want it to continue.

One may achieve personal and financial success via the business and emotional support one can get from these events, which goes beyond just boosting confidence.

Shape up

If you are in good health, you can do anything with confidence. If you're not, just surviving may be difficult. Being physically healthy is crucial for both your mental and emotional health. The simplest, most readily available, and least expensive antidepressant is exercise. Therefore, get up and start exercising rather than merely reading about how healthy it is for your body and mind.

When I was a kid, I used to hear my father's cigar-smoking friend say, "Kid, ya ain't got your health, ya ain't got nothing," in a throaty smoker's voice. It simply felt nasty at the moment. After a few years (and a few "procedures"), I've come to the conclusion that even though he disregarded his own advice, he was entirely correct. One of the most crucial components of a self-assured and happy existence is being healthy and encouraging people you love to do the same.

Given the obesity crisis and the widespread media coverage of how leading a healthy lifestyle not only extends life but also improves one's character in several ways, I find it astounding that so few people take adequate care of themselves. Many people I know care for their pets better than they do for themselves. I love my dogs dearly, and I am aware that they would go hungry if I am unable to open cans, therefore I need to be healthy in order to take care of them.

Even the necessities of life seem burdensome when we are unhealthy or out of shape. Chronic or even life-threatening illnesses might cause some individuals to exercise more than healthy but sedentary persons. Most individuals are motivated to start exercising when they finally understand that without good physical health, their circumstances will not get any better any time soon, and their aspirations may never come true. You must maintain the engine that drives your thoughts and ideas.

Believe in yourself

The enteric nervous system, as it is known, is a form of thinking mechanism that scientists have found operates inside our digestive systems.

We've all experienced intuitions or "gut emotions," but many people are unaware of how much they rely on these experiences. Picking lottery numbers isn't the point of intuition; it's just another kind of information to take into account. It is a method of hearing what is happening inside of oneself, and it may assist you in coping with many kinds of concerns as well as despair and worry.

If you disagree with the value of your own intuition, consider how often you have had an idea but ignored it, only to wish you had. The truth is that your body often has more knowledge than your mind, if not more. The key is to figure out how to tune in to that really useful aspect of yourself, and the first step is to have faith that it exists.
Although going with your gut instincts might be a bit frightening at first (and you might worry if others will start treating you like you're from another planet), doing so can be really beneficial for managing life's continual changes and is mostly harmless.

You may discover fresh insights or get solutions to problems by using your intuition.You must be at least somewhat at ease, in touch with your emotions, and free of emotional control in order to engage in the intuitive process.

The best way to get started is to take a deep breath, close your eyes, and focus on your internal experience. Sometimes concentrating on your breathing is beneficial. Once you've done it a few hundred times, it is as easy as it seems. If you feel like you're doing everything wrong and nothing is working, try not to become irritated. Be kind to yourself and use this strategy as often as you can. Everybody is intuitive. You only need to tune in.

Trust your gut feelings, as well as your ambitions to excel or build the next Facebook. Pay attention to the inner voice that encourages you.

These are various ways that our intuition shows itself inside of us. It cannot be programmed like a computer. It's more like a process of strengthening a mental muscle. Simply take it slower and let it happen organically.

Intuition is a tool used by musicians, authors, and artists. It is used by parents to keep their kids safe, and every day, billions of individuals base their choices on their gut sensations. A powerful technique for improving your life and your relationships is to trust your intuition.

Learn to celebrate small victories you make

Contrary to popular belief, millions of individuals have discovered that confidence is not a prerequisite for success. This is due to the fact that achieving success in any one aspect of your life—no matter how small—has an impact on all the others. As I like to refer to them, little wins might include everything from locating a fantastic parking spot to purchasing a lottery ticket and winning $10. You have to take them in if you want to convert these little victories into confidence. That is to say, you have to feel all the feelings that come with achievement.

You may educate your brain cells and provide them with the most addictive force in nature, intermittent positive reinforcement, by enabling yourself to feel successful. Your subconscious will seek out that sensation as often as it can whenever you offer it something to feel good about. If you recognize and appreciate your daily accomplishments, no matter how tiny, you can't help but feel better about yourself and want more.

Even the seemingly inconsequential or time-wasting little activities may help you accomplish your most important objectives.

You may educate your brain to desire success to happen again, for instance, by really believing in yourself that the presentation you just made was a home run, even if there were only four people in the room. Whether on purpose or not, you will bring it about.

You may permanently ingrain something nice in your mind by telling yourself that you accomplished something good. Imagine it as being archived on the hard drive of your memory. It's there, just like the file you've been looking for on your computer. Once you locate it, you will always be aware of its location and operation.

The programming for such feelings is similarly accessible if you are aware of how to succeed or what it feels like to be confident since they are stored in your brain and you will remember where to retrieve them.

If you can't even get out of bed in the morning, you're not going to experience the success of going for a stroll or planting some flowers. For some people who are suffering, even the thought of a modest win seems out of reach. As a result, you must suitably scale down your ambitions. Consider getting out of bed, taking a shower, and reading the newspaper while sitting in your backyard as little victories. Once you start taking that stroll and life stops seeming insurmountable, you will have pushed yourself to accomplish just a little bit more each day.

Success occurs. Every day, it occurs to everyone.
Opening our eyes and giving ourselves a high five can be all it takes to see it

materialize in our life. The purest type of self-esteem comes from developing your own confidence via your own achievement.

Build a confidence circle

Group exercises may sometimes help you feel more empowered, and some of them can really boost your self-assurance. Most are enjoyable, and a few may have significant, uplifting effects. Five to ten persons are required for this specific exercise:

The participants form a circle around the center person who is seated (hand holding is optional). Each individual seated outside the circle will compliment the person within it on a number of different attributes. After everyone has completed speaking in the circle, the person in the center turns to the person next to him in the circle and relates what he recalls hearing.

For everyone to be able to see what they learned and what they missed, there should be a scribe taking notes or videotaping the activity. After everyone has had a chance to experience being the receiver, do this section of the activity. This is the trick: Your beliefs about yourself are based on the things you can repeat and recall.
We are aware of this since you were able to accept them and relate to them. You could be surprised to hear things that were said about you that you didn't believe others would. You may boost your confidence and even develop some in areas where you'd want to have more with the aid of this procedure.

When you don't feel at the top of your game
or like you don't deserve the praise, you find
it difficult to hold onto the praises.
It's vital to remember that these
encouraging words originated from
individuals who may perceive you
differently than you do. An important
technique for being your best and boosting
your confidence is getting an outside
viewpoint.

To be completely honest, when I initially
completed this exercise, the only
compliment I could recall was that I
received a number of positive comments
about my sense of humor. Although I was
still very young, I did recognize that I ought

to have been able to take in more good information, and this exercise motivated me to do exactly that. I acquired the skill of listening to compliments that were said to and about me. Even though I still find it surprising when someone praises my writing or my speaking, and even though I may not always recognize the positive aspects, I try to take the praise to heart. I firmly feel that doing so improves both my performance and self-worth.

Over the course of a year, repeat this practice multiple times to boost your confidence.

Don't lower yourself by raising your voice

Verbal abuse is one of the worst things you can do in a relationship, whether it's personal or professional. Simply said, it makes you seem to be a bully who is insecure. The fact is that individuals who are self-assured seldom need to shout.

Fortunately, shouting might be among the simplest habits to break. In situations like these, it might be helpful to reflect on the past to see if anything in your past contributed to the development of the undesirable habit.

Maybe you grew up in a household where screaming and insults were normal and tolerated as a part of family life. Since they are not consciously impacted by it, many individuals fail to notice anything wrong with it. Unfortunately, there are considerable unconscious impacts. Take a look at how it affected your sense of self and level of confidence.

People who are exposed to verbal abuse at work or at home are less secure than the rest of us. It's not a wonderful way to go through life wondering whether you'll still be in your relationship or have a job tomorrow.

Setting a good example for others is one of the most powerful strategies you can use to stop this undesirable habit. If you shout, you are encouraging (and teaching others a lesson) to do the same. It could be time to modify the cycle if it has persisted for a few generations. It's not as challenging as you may imagine.

To start, you must become conscious of the habit. Starting with oneself is a smart idea. You may stop yourself by realizing that you do sometimes become overpowering.

Those who are really bold and who genuinely want their lives to improve will also provide their family members, friends, and/or colleagues permission to gently remind them when they participate in loud talk that shouting isn't something they want to do any more.

It may take some time for you to recall the reasons you desire to control your temper and refrain from verbally abusing others.

Simple methods like taking a stroll, walking outside, breathing deeply, or shutting your eyes and imagining placing yourself in a better emotional state will help you reach that peace.

Stopping verbal abuse in its tracks is difficult when you get hot, but the outcomes are worthwhile. In this situation, repetition really is the mother of invention, and the more times you attempt to break the pattern, the simpler it will be.

Your life will improve both at home and elsewhere if you can learn to avoid the negative energy of verbal abuse. Because you are handling life in an adult way and receiving respect from others, you will also earn self-respect and confidence.

So keep an eye on yourself and practice speaking in a way that will make your family and friends accept your chats and ideas. You never have to degrade yourself by speaking louder.

Do the things you fear

I spent a year in art school just to be sure—I have no skill in the visual arts. My first day of sketching class stands out in my memory. I had everything I needed, including butcher paper and a tackle box full of other fishing instruments that I had never used before.

I picked a seat in the room with decent lighting while walking to class, my shoulder-length hair flowing in the Berkeley breeze (really, it was near a window, and I adore fresh air). While I awaited the professor to place a vase or other kind of still life on the pedestal in the middle of the room, I set up my easel and unlocked my little box of paints. When a young lady in a kimono entered the room, climbed upon the stage, and removed her robe, I wasn't paying any attention. Naturally, it caught my eye, but not for the reason you would suppose. I was going to flunk my first lesson and was really terrified since I knew I couldn't draw a human.

How to handle difficult conversation

The only effective approach to manage conflict is to engage in it. Most people avoid having awkward talks because, well, they're uncomfortable. Unfortunately, delaying the pain and maybe fostering animosity are the results of avoiding a difficult circumstance. Being confident in both yourself and your communication abilities is crucial in this situation.

Here are some suggestions on how to approach and successfully carry on a conversation about a challenging subject.

Open the channels of communication and get feedback from the other side in order to best determine a fair solution to your problem. By doing this, you are demonstrating that you have sufficient confidence and care to accept the risk. Additionally, because you started the process, it gives you a little additional strength. Additionally, doing so will significantly lessen the other person's defensiveness and increase his willingness to cooperate.

Once the discussion starts, thank the other person for agreeing to speak with you. At the beginning and the conclusion of the conversation, thank him for his time. It will turn the conversation into a team effort and make him feel as if he has contributed. Additionally, by reducing defensiveness, it will make the subsequent uncomfortable dialogue simpler.

You may save a lot of hassle by giving the talk a time restriction. You should converse, but be careful not to exhaust one another. The longest most individuals can tolerate is between 30 and 60 minutes. If you need to continue the talk, schedule a time to do so within the following few days so that nothing is left unfinished.

You may let each other know that you really "understood" (or didn't understand) how each of you are feeling by learning to paraphrase each other's statements by sharing what you heard one another say. At first, this could seem a bit onerous, but by preserving clarity, it benefits everyone. Additionally, it will provide you both the assurance that the talk is moving in the direction you want.

Compromise is the key to resolution, and how you get at it will decide how satisfied you are with the result. Giving someone what they need or want does not equate to giving up or caving. Your attitude in this situation is crucial. Being certain without coming off as arrogant can help you both feel that you received what you wanted and that you can put any bad sentiments that may have developed behind you.

Making a list of the questions you have and the actions you would want the other person to do might be helpful; it is usually simpler to retain information when it is in writing and to remain on topic. Additionally, it aids in ensuring that you address the whole problem rather than just a portion of it.

Accept being incorrect. Conversations that are challenging don't always go as planned. Sometimes it's acceptable to modify your viewpoint or offer an apology. It would only lead to further strife to harbor resentment because you didn't obtain what you thought you wanted.
Being incorrect doesn't bother confident individuals; in fact, the majority see it as a chance to improve for the future.

You will be able to confirm what you already know and discover what you don't by seeking out and valuing professional opinion. Always keep in mind that no one individual has all the knowledge, thus consulting many sources is perfectly acceptable. It's also completely fine to ask a third person to mediate your talk if it turns into an argument. Take the time to evaluate what a colleague, professor, therapist, or other professional has to say whether he supports or refutes your views. You'll learn more as a result.

You will find it much simpler to diffuse situations if you are aware of the emotional aspect of communication. Make sure you're speaking from the heart, but don't allow your sentiments to control you, since difficult talks may elicit a wide range of emotions. Contrast how you are feeling with how you believe the other person is feeling about you. By doing so, the likelihood of sentiments of guilt or wrath will be reduced and the communication will remain clear.

Consolidate the achievements and reiterate your commitment to taking things ahead once everyone has had a chance to speak and agreements have been reached. After the conversation, evaluate the decision you made (even if it was only to continue discussing at a later time), come to an agreement on the result, and let the other person or individuals know that you are open for more discussions if needed. Finally, don't penalize them for bringing up a challenging subject.

One of the most useful skills you may have to boost and keep up your self-confidence is the ability to conduct a good uncomfortable discussion. Although most people find this difficult, anybody can accomplish it with

enough time, effort, and practice. The initial
stage of discomfort must be overcome, and
you must be aware that once your problems
are on the table, your life will become lighter
and more joyful.

Avoid critical comment

People will avoid you if you say harsh things to them often enough, and eventually they won't want to connect or contact you. You won't have an emotional support system left at that time, and self-confidence will be as elusive as a shooting star.

We can all be so nitpicky that people we work with and care about flee or cover their ears and mutter, "La la la," so they won't hear us. When criticisms are a way of life, people just tune them out.

When you are continually criticizing, the individual who seems to be benefiting from your wise counsel could be behaving politely to get you to quit as soon as possible. In reality, you are pushing this individual away even if you are attempting to assist. Additionally, if your counsel is dismissed, you will feel that it is not valued or taken into consideration. No matter how accurate your message is, it can't do your confidence any good if it's not heard.

Consider your words carefully and consider how you would react before telling someone how you feel (or simply telling her off) in order to break this vicious loop. She will be tampered with if you are. We don't do this easy thought process nearly enough.

Most of the time, when we believe we have a suggestion for how someone may improve upon something, we feel obligated to share it with him. However, the reality is that whomever it is, he is probably doing his best, so informing him that it might have been done better would simply make him less enthusiastic.

Wait until everyone has left the room before saying anything like, "I really enjoyed what you had to say, but I don't believe everyone understood you. If you genuinely think your feedback will enhance someone's life, behavior, or job, wait until everyone has left the room. If you're interested, I have a suggestion that may be helpful to you.

People will be more receptive to what you have to say if you communicate in a manner that doesn't make them feel judged or denigrated. This will advance not just their skill set but also yours. It really boosts your confidence to know that you can see things that others may not, and to have that vision validated.

The proverb "It's not what it seems" has a lot of truth to it not only what you say, but also how. No matter how wise you are, someone's capacity to absorb information will be lowered if she believes you are about to blast her. Never dismiss or judge someone without giving them the benefit of the doubt. If you disagree with someone, that is OK as long as you do it politely. Additionally, remember to smile and talk in a kind tone. A bit more than half of communication is visual, and almost half is tonal. The other person will understand that you are coming from a loving place if you speak in a calm, honest manner. This is the language of the self-assured.

Give out some energy

Your capacity to increase the emotions of a friend, family member, or colleague when they are struggling is a more effective treatment than Prozac. It makes sense to seek out someone you are confident in and who cares about you when life is throwing sand in your face. It might significantly affect how you feel if that individual can really help you by offering emotional support and encouraging words. It almost seems too easy. If you have trouble offering or receiving that type of help, you should examine your mental condition and make a few changes. Perhaps you are transferring your mistrust of the world or your worry about your boss' unfair remarks, but it won't do you any good. Giving and getting supportive feedback from people closest to you will be beneficial.

We all do it occasionally—normal, it's but it's also harmful and will undermine whatever confidence you may have after a trying day. Make a sincere assessment of both your capacity for receiving positive reinforcement and your capacity for releasing unpleasant feelings. Check yourself out because using emotions as a weapon, even minimally, is a terrific way to start a conflict.

Your agony will be reduced by the peace that comes over your body and mind when someone is there to make everything great. Additionally, you will be able to think more clearly on the best course of action once you are feeling better.

Your uneasiness will diminish if you have a solid game plan, and you'll feel more confident about handling the circumstance. Look, the world isn't fair, and we could all use a little encouragement now and again (pom-poms optional). It is a gift you give to the person who isn't feeling at the top of her game to be there for someone in need, and it is reciprocated in many ways.

The most evident is that both of you will feel a brighter mood in the air.

She will feel much more encouraged if you say something like, "I know you're anxious, but we'll get through this together [or as a team]," or "You've always landed on your feet, so why should this time be any different?" It's okay to just be there while she pouts a bit. No matter where our sadness originates, keep in mind that we all need to process it.

Your life has mostly turned out well.

Another extremely useful approach is to remind yourself and everyone around you of this while also reflecting on your past experiences and where you are right now. This universe may be all about receiving or offering an emotional lift from someone who is on your side. And my, does it feel good.

Develop your inner strength

When the going gets tough and you contemplate cashing in, you turn to the power inside you. You'll feel like you can handle whatever life throws at you if you use your most inventive inner resources to "pick yourself up by the bootstraps." Wouldn't it be fantastic if we could move our strengths around? We all have strengths in different areas. Imagine using all of your brainpower to raise a sofa or directing all of your emotional strength into your problem-solving abilities. You would be unstoppable, and those who reach greatness are just that. The only thing that separates them from you is that they are aware of how to access and use their abilities. The good news is that you can learn this particular skill set.

The ability to summon inner power when necessary is something the greats have learnt to achieve first by having faith in their own abilities. That often indicates that they have sufficiently honed, honed, and polished their skill set to know they can always think of a response or plan their way out of a pickle.

People who seem to be good at flying by their seats have often invested a lot of time in their skills.Only because it is a step in the process does it seem simple. Your strength doesn't want (or need) to be sapped by pointless conflict. Making things seem simple is thus a deliberate change of attitude. Don't waste your time; do what you can in the most effective manner you are capable of, and have faith that the outcomes will be positive.

Since bravado is a waste of time, inner power is pure and manifests itself without it. Inner power is a silent triumph that doesn't call for parades or even public acclaim (thought that seldom hurts).

Success is generally enough of a reward when you know something needs your full effort.

Getting in touch with your inner power is a little bit of an art. Others need to condition themselves with speech, imagery, or even exercise, while other individuals need to first calm themselves in order to locate their reservoir.

Hindsight is a fantastic tool for digging through your own toolbox. You will have more resources to draw on if you remind yourself that you have overcome worse and that you will overcome the current problem. Even if the new problem is completely unexpected or strange, the knowledge that you have overcome far greater problems is a fantastic confidence builder.

You always have access to your inner power. Consider it your psyche's Swiss Army Knife: All the equipment you need is in your pocket. You just need to reach inside and pull them out. I am aware that we sometimes find it easy to forget to utilize our internal resources when we are under stress, even though that is precisely the moment when we need them the most.

So, the next time you feel overwhelmed or anxious, remember how you handled similar situations in the past and have faith in your ability to handle this one as well. You already possess all of the inner power you need, in actuality.

The greats have discovered that having faith in one's ability to succeed is one of the first steps towards finding inner strength when it is required. That often indicates they've worked on honing their skill set well enough to know they can always think of an answer or devise a solution to a problem.

Those who seem to be good at "flying by the seat of their trousers" have frequently invested a lot of time on their skills.

Because it is a step in the process, it merely seems to be simple.

You don't want (or need) to engage in needless conflict since it will weaken your strength. Making things seem simple is really a deliberate attitude modification. Don't squander your energy; instead, do what you can to the best of your ability and have faith in the success of the outcome. Bravado is unnecessary since inner power is pure and appears without it. Inner fortitude is a quiet triumph that doesn't need parades or even outer recognition (thought that seldom hurts).

Success is often sufficient compensation when you know something needs your utmost effort.

It takes a certain amount of skill to gather your inner power. Some individuals need to be still in order to locate their reservoir, while others need to prepare themselves via interaction, imagination, or even physical activity.

Hindsight is a fantastic tool for accessing your particular repertoire of techniques. You'll have more resources to draw on if you remind yourself that you've overcome worse and that you'll get through whatever problem you're now experiencing. Even if the new problem is wholly unexpected or strange, the knowledge that you have overcome far greater problems is a fantastic confidence builder.

A resource you always have at your disposal is your inner strength.

Consider it the Swiss Army Knife of your mind: You already have all the equipment you need in your pocket. To remove them, all you need to do is reach inside and pull. I am aware that sometimes when we are under stress, it is easy to forget to utilize our own resources, even if that is precisely the moment when we need them the most. Therefore, the next time you are worried or feeling overwhelmed, reflect on how you handled such situations in the past and have faith in your ability to handle this one as well. The fact is that you already possess all of the inner power you need.

Enlightenment

There aren't many who spring to mind when we think about enlightened people: We have been enlightened and led to define our lives by spiritual leaders like Jesus, Buddha, and Moses, business titans like Warren Buffett, Lee Iacocca, and Bill Gates, and musicians like Elvis Presley, The Beatles, and Ozzie Osborne (well, maybe not him). Our capacity to experience enlightenment keeps us steadfast in our judgments and choices.

We pay attention to what the wise have to say because they have gained credibility through time. The spiritual masters developed over a long period of time, and we have had plenty of time to absorb their teachings. Although they have had far less time to penetrate our psyches, the masters of the arts and business are gaining more and more respect. Why else would Warren Buffett be referred to as "The Oracle of Omaha"?

These folks attained enlightenment via hard work; you may do the same. There are many distinct sorts of enlightenment, which is even better news given that you don't have to be a master (or dead) to get it. Thus, there is no need to contrast oneself with a charismatic religious figure or a dejected rock star.

When business is sluggish, the wise leader understands how to increase confidence. When pupils need to feel better about themselves in order to achieve, the wise teacher is aware of it. The wise friend understands when someone needs a shoulder to weep on and that no words are necessary since it simply seems safer to talk about our problems with someone else. We should all have our own unique enlightenments, as we all do. There is no need for you to feel bad about missing one or two steps since no one can be enlightened in all areas. Would a wise person even have such thoughts, I mean, really?

The truth of enlightenment is as follows: It is a lifetime endeavor, and as you struggle to achieve it, you will only become more self-assured.

Although your ideas may sway with the wind, your awakened soul will never waver. GURU has always made me think of the phrase "Gee-You-Are-You."

Love yourself

One of the most neglected sources of our self-esteem may be self-love. We are capable of being more harsh on ourselves than anybody else. You may conserve your energy for the crucial aspects of life and maintain your confidence by consciously taking care of yourself and avoiding the trap of self-deprecation.

Look, narcissism and self-love are quite different things. There is no place in the hearts of narcissistic people because they are in love with themselves rather than anybody or anything else. However, individuals who have worked hard and come to love themselves are not only able to receive good energy from other people, but are also able to return it tenfold.

There will always be a reason we don't feel worthy of any love, whether it comes from inside, from another person, or even from God, so when we don't love ourselves, our confidence can't grow. People who beat themselves up in this manner have incredibly challenging relationships and lives. Despite the fact that this is a very challenging circumstance, there are a variety of ways you may start to love and trust yourself.

No one will be able to provide you with a course correction that you will hear if you are adversely judging your own manner of being. This one needs to originate in your own heart and mind. It is a life-changing process to come to the understanding that you don't like your life, and then to delve deeper and find out that what you don't like is who you have become.

The good news in this situation is that you may be quite different from the person you have become from who you really are. To ensure that you are living your fundamental principles, you must reconnect with them. If not, it will disrupt the area of your brain that controls self-esteem, and you won't be able to explain why you feel the way you do.

It's similar to changing a tire to stop doing things that make you loathe or find it difficult to love oneself.

You must first pause to evaluate the damage. What tire is that? Is it really level, or is it simply low? Make sure you have the

power and resources to address the issue
after you've identified and acknowledged its
existence. So you check the spare tire in the
trunk and make sure you have a jack and a
lug wrench. First check your spare before
attempting to fix a flat emotional psyche:
Can you alter your habits enough to have a
big influence on your life and self-love?
Make sure you have the resources you need,
including a solid network of support, a basic
understanding of personal development,
and possibly a skilled therapist to guide you
through the challenging times ahead. If not,
you must develop a plan and system for your
own personal development. Without it,
getting there will be far more challenging, if
not impossible.

With the right skills, you may improve your relationships with people around you and learn to love yourself, both of which will help you feel better about yourself.

Always appreciate yourself

You can't help but feel more self-assured when you're content with who you are as a person. The key to happiness is appreciating what you already have, not obtaining all you want.

Even if you haven't yet accomplished your objectives, you can and need to be content while working toward them. If not, you could be moving in the wrong path and your subconscious is trying to warn you something isn't quite right. These signals that emerge from our unconscious need to be heard (and maybe translated), since they contain a wealth of knowledge that we probably aren't completely aware of.

Additionally, as we become older, our sense of satisfaction alters. When we are fed, clothed, and loved as children, we feel fairly wonderful. Teenagers want acceptance and the feeling that they are cool enough. When we eventually reach adulthood, our sense of contentment often shifts as we start to weigh the benefits and drawbacks of things like marriage, having kids, working for someone else, or establishing our own business—all of which we think will take us to the pinnacle of personal fulfillment. The issue is that our wants and aspirations often change as we age, which is why it is so crucial to be confident in the decisions you make while creating your life, regardless of your age.

A family may not work for you if you are aware that you are not a "child person," even if it is very satisfying for many others. You must be confident that it is the best choice for you, even if your parents may have done it and everyone else may be doing it.

You won't be happy if you make significant choices in life because someone you are with or connected to desires it for you. It's fair that you don't want to let your loved ones down, but the fact is that if you're unsure that you're making the proper choice, speak to someone about it, write it down, and give it a lot of thought before taking a step ahead. Because these decisions will probably affect you for the rest of your life, maintain your self-assurance.

It's crucial to realize that confidence affects satisfaction in a similar manner to how doing good for others fosters self-respect. It is impossible to avoid feeling better about your life and the people in it when you are doing something that makes you feel good and that you think is the correct thing to do.

Looking for satisfaction could also require taking a close look at what you already possess. To understand that everything she had ever desired was there in her own backyard, Dorothy had to go to Oz. After encounters with flying monkeys, lions, tigers, and bears as well as witches, she ultimately realized that contentment comes

from enjoying what you currently have
rather than pursuing your goals. And Toto
as well.

Trust yourself

Because not having it immediately
undermines your confidence, you must start
by giving yourself trust.

Trust that you are here for the right reasons
and that people around you value your full
involvement in life.

Ask the people you know and who care
about you whether you have had an impact
on their life if you are unable to determine
this for yourself.

It is difficult to believe that we deserve to be
here or that wonderful things will happen to
us when we are unable to see our value in
the world. Receiving approval from
individuals close to you will make it easier
for you to realize how much you have

improved their lives and possibly even the globe at large. Consider the aspects of your life that you are proud of.

There are plenty of them, but you may have to take some time to recall how much you enjoyed and accomplished in renovating that old antique dresser or how once you truly helped someone (or yourself) save a lot of money with straightforward advice. You deserve to be trusted since you have amazing intuition, but you have to locate that confidence inside yourself in order to boost it.

Heart of Gratitude

Better years than worse years exist. The economic crisis that has led to millions of job losses and millions more living in worry that they may follow suit has made the last few years more challenging. Many people are having trouble finding things for which to be thankful and feel confident about in the years ahead. Add to that the lost funds, lost houses, and children moving back into their parents' homes (perhaps with their own kids).

Well, if you just relocated or welcomed relatives, your home may be more crowded, but you also have more love. Some individuals have the good fortune to have family members they really love spending time with, in which case having them live with you is more advantageous than inconvenient. Even if you don't really like the circumstances, they won't last forever, and as those of us who have experienced similar circumstances know, in the end they will leave you with some priceless memories. Additionally, having an additional set of hands while you're carrying in the groceries and an extra confidence boost when you need it are both side benefits.

I've heard that for individuals who are unemployed or making less money (which would be the majority of us), after a time of getting accustomed to living on less, life is pretty much the same. People may feel a little more worn out at the end of the day due to difficulties with budgeting or taking on a second job, but they are also thankful that they can again support their family once more.

Many of the folks I know are retraining themselves. Some people may not find it all that appealing to return to college or a trade school in their middle years, but I did it through a couple of recessions and I will always be happy I took the decision. Greater self-esteem, a reliable income, and the satisfaction of doing what you want to do are the outcomes, despite the intimidating notion and terrifying burden. Returning to school is not a sign of failure; rather, it demonstrates to others and to oneself that you are resilient enough to handle challenges and creative enough to find solutions. You are more than just a survivor;

you are a thriver, which should give you greater confidence.

This mindset might assist you in taking stock of what you have and your untapped potential if life is dragging you down in any way. We are all aware that hardship makes us stronger, but for those who have been struggling with the effects of the economy, it may be difficult to see beyond the setbacks and imagine a more promising future. Perhaps not in the next year, but sooner or later, things will improve, and when they do, I believe you will see that your priorities have changed as well. The love we have in our lives will always be the most significant aspect of life. Being thankful for it can help you feel a kind of confidence that nothing else can.

Building Confidence in your Workplace

In order to be effective, confidence-building programs must contain instruction on emotional intelligence. Contrary to conventional belief, emotional people are passionate individuals who bring about change. They enact change and upend the status quo. Their enthusiasm breeds perseverance, and they provide a healthy dose of vigor and productivity to the businesses they work for. Of fact, many company owners and top managers believe that emotions are undesirable and that everything should be calm, detached, and objective.

They also spend a tremendous amount of time and money attempting to energize staff because they want them to be driven and enthusiastic about their work. Even if you had the power, it would be counterproductive to exclude emotions from the job since passion is a good sort of emotion. Helping individuals feel comfortable expressing their feelings in a sensible way as opposed to ranting is what works best.
Fostering confidence while preventing a lack of it from bankrupting the firm is a problem for corporations.

There is little doubt that unpleasant feelings may make workers behave erratically, indulge in blaming and name-calling, and eventually undermine management's objectives. A business risks losing excellent personnel as well as good clients and consumers if negative and unresolved emotions are not handled. The business might enter a downward spiral from which it could never emerge. Whether they like it or not, today's leaders spend half of their time counseling their employees, so it's critical that they do a good job of it and provide their team members a positive sense of self and their organization.

Plan B

Having a "Plan B" is an excellent concept since many things don't go as smoothly as we would want them to. Fallback plans are a typical trait among individuals who are incredibly self-assured and can't help but make you feel better about the outcome of any circumstance.

Anyone who has experienced more than one setback in life can attest to the fact that having a backup plan may have saved her skin at least once or twice. I'm a big one \for contingency preparations. A Plan B is necessary if you are an entrepreneur, work in the arts or media, or if you put all of your eggs in one basket.

You feel safer in the world knowing that you have a condo to go to if you lose the farm. I know many individuals who own mobile homes, and one of the justifications for their ownership is that it serves as their "in case" house, as they humorously put it. Many individuals who had them during the most recent major earthquake in Los Angeles were quite appreciative, and those of us without them were jealous.

Making any kind of supplemental income stream is also an excellent idea given the state of the global economy.

Even if their present role is eliminated, the jeweler who is also a superb designer or constructor, the computer nerd who can also teach, or the PR professional who is a secret author, may all continue to prosper.

Backup strategies don't necessarily need to be original concepts—I still draw on everything I've done in some way.

I've improved my public speaking skills because of my time spent performing guitar on stage, which helps me as a radio presenter. I put a lot of effort into my songs and poetry, which helped them develop into books and columns. I have the knowledge to assist others in streamlining their businesses because of the years I spent operating my own. And thanks to all of my experiences, I am now a self-assured and prosperous therapist. You can develop and use each talent and skill you possess. Not that I'd ever want to spend eight weeks on a tour bus with six stinky dudes again, but if I had to, I could still make a living by strumming and humming.

Another positive aspect of this situation is that sometimes your primary strategy and backup plan may both succeed. I continue to provide advice, advise, write, and deliver speeches to audiences all around the globe. I spent more time writing and doing counseling during years when the speaking business was relatively sluggish (such as those after 9/11 and the subsequent financial crisis). In the interim between publications, I focused more on my radio program, business consultancy, and volunteer work. Having a variety of possibilities gives you the impression that you would have other jobs that would more than cover the void of any one item where to go.

So use some imagination. Take a look at your prior successes and your present abilities. Just an idea away from a Plan B. By the way, although Plan B works in life, it doesn't work in love. Having a backup partner won't do anything except strain your existing union and make everyone unhappy.

Dealing with disappointment

Things just don't work out sometimes. Murphy's Law may seem to be the rule in your environment, leaving you disillusioned with life and possibly even with yourself. The majority of people believe that self-confident individuals never have to deal with disappointment. Everyone reacts to failure in a different way, and those who exhibit confident behaviors may not be derailed from their goals as quickly as those who experience moderate levels of self-doubt. The good news is that everyone can learn how to deal with disappointment better, and when you do, a side effect is that your confidence grows.

When people are disappointed, their emotions may range from staying in bed for days on end (which is not very practical if you have a life) to perhaps feeling depressed and becoming less productive. There will be emotional suffering and a loss of energy if you take disappointment and use it against yourself or blame yourself for it.

When things don't turn out the way we want them to, we all need to develop our own coping mechanisms. This is the material that life is composed of, from broken relationships to lost business prospects or financial losses. You won't have the chance to move on from your disappointment or, at the very least, learn from it if you pull the covers up over your head.

An aware person experiences the typical melancholy that comes with a setback; a confident person expresses those emotions in a healthy way and comes up with a strategy to make himself feel better. This often entails some kind of emotional or physical release, such as cleaning the home or yard, seeing a therapist, working out, or anything else that enables one to let go and so process his emotions. A further activity is taken to assist counteract the discontent.

Although you may not be able to reverse the original disappointment, you can focus your efforts elsewhere and boost your mood by making progress on other areas. Whatever is going on in your life, doing something positive like organizing your sock drawer, trimming the flowers, or creating the next great American book will help you feel better about yourself and your circumstances.

The wind gets taken out of our sails by disappointment. You may either decide to take up your paddle and begin paddling for land while sitting calmly in the center of your remorse. I'm unsure whether you'll arrive on a desolate island or a lush tropical paradise. However, remaining still would undoubtedly convert you into fish bait, making starting to row your only viable option.

It's very normal to feel briefly dissatisfied with your circumstances. Staying there is just and simply a decision. I'd rather try 100 times and fail than never try at all. There are several methods to make things happen, and life is too short to dwell in disappointment. You are capable of doing it.

Don't be intimidated by Age

When I was a youngster, I spotted a sign at Knott's Berry Farm that said, "Don't regret becoming older; there are few individuals who have that pleasure." I have always kept that in mind and incorporated it into my set of core values. It gives me a positive outlook on the future and helps me enjoy my time in the world with minimal regrets.

Everyone has to be born at some point, and hating your age will have a negative impact on other aspects of your life and lower your self-esteem. Regarding your age and identity, you are what you are. The only way to live a full life is to accept that. You miss

out on the present, the assurance that comes
with experience, and the knowledge that
comes with age if you lament your youth.

I wholeheartedly agree with James Taylor's
famous line, "The key of life is appreciating
the passage of time." There must be more
than one secret, but this one is very useful.
You will go to sleep with regrets and wake
up anxious if you can't cherish each day and
get the most out of it that you can. More
happiness and self-assurance will come
from believing that you are with the right
people, at the right age, in the right location
than from listening to a roomful of self-help
CDs. I don't want to grow up to be a cranky
old guy. I want a "good enough" standard of
living. I put it that way because I understand
that getting older might have some

negatives and I try to keep my expectations in check since I detest being let down. I anticipate having a few physical problems; they could make me go more slowly, but I won't allow them to stop me. In addition, isn't slowing down the ideal method to observe your surroundings?

No one leaves this place alive, so you simply have to decide to make the most of your current situation. If you don't, regardless of your age, the happiness you may be experiencing will turn into woulda, shoulda, and couldas. Be true to yourself. Be what you are. Men wearing T-shirts with slogans like "Old Guys Rule" make me smile.

The men that wear them not only have the attitude of "I may be older, but I don't act like it," but they also have the sense of humor needed to pull them out of bed every morning.

I know too many individuals who didn't start living until they were in their 40s or 50s, and they are benefiting greatly from the second part of their lives. Please be aware that you could also fit that description.

Change the way you think

It may be really beneficial to change the way you think.

Unfortunately, sometimes it requires a traumatic loss, like getting abruptly fired from your job or having your girlfriend break up with you. When something of that scale happens, you are forced to reconsider your life.

Rewiring your brain processes is necessary when you want to make a substantial change in your life, like quitting drinking and using up all your money. The result is that you build new, more advantageous neural pathways in your brain, which alters how you think and feel for the better by causing you to think and feel differently.

You won't be able to maintain your transformation, attract new connections, or create new possibilities if you attempt to disregard the changes in your thinking. Only if you have the determination to adopt a new outlook on life will these alterations be attainable. It may be really motivating to realize that your previous way of thinking can be holding you back.

Being self-assured and seeing that a change has to be made is what leads to the decision to build a better life for yourself and the people you care about. Even when doing extremely private actions, like altering the way you speak or mastering the art of fair conflict resolution and temper management,

which may need for training or therapy,
others are inextricably involved.
The help of friends and family may be quite
important while trying to improve anything.
In order to get the help you need, set aside
some time to strengthen your connections.
If you want to understand what your loved
ones think of you, you may have to take a
chance and ask some challenging questions.
Making mental and emotional changes may
be quite challenging for those who are alone.

A support group might be beneficial if you
realize that your old way of life isn't working
and you're having trouble figuring out how
to change. The people there may help you by
clarifying and demonstrating new habits,
and you can also discover things about
yourself that can be hard to view from an

unbiased standpoint. Just keep in mind that not everyone in every organization is on the same page, so you should be selective when choosing someone to sponsor or mentor you.

Most people are aware that change is a constant in life. We often adjust rather easily to changes in the environment or even in other individuals. When we have to change how we live our lives, it might be much more difficult. You can be sure you didn't make this choice quickly. Even though you didn't want to do it at first, it will be simpler to accept once you see how important it is.

Whatever your requirements, keep in mind that everything begins with you, and making significant adjustments is really a present you are providing to those who care about you as well as yourself.

Take Risk

You won't be let down if your expectations are modest, but you also won't receive much else. Although having preferences rather than expectations or having low expectations of either oneself or others is emotionally safer, what does it truly bring you?

Setting oneself up for disappointment is different from handling it well. Applying for American Idol when you've never performed well in front of an audience can be a setup: In addition to being let down, you could also disgrace yourself in front of a large number of people (which might make you seek comfort in the Haagen-Dazs container bottom).

It's okay to put a bit if you're dealing with disappointment properly; it's normal to reconsider after a demoralizing experience. It also doesn't imply that when you feel like hiding in a hole, you have to fake happiness. It does imply that you must draw conclusions from your experience and take action to improve future encounters. Keeping things in perspective may just entail having faith that there will be another chance.

You must keep in mind that whenever you put yourself out there, whether it's for romantic reasons or to perform in front of an audience, you run the danger of your "crowd" not reacting as you would want.

Additionally, keep in mind that taking chances is something that not many people do, therefore it speaks well of you. Someone who goes into combat without considering the possibility of major damage or death is not considered courageous; rather, it is someone who is afraid but moves on nevertheless.

Such bravery is admirable. It could take a close friend or family member to remind you that even if things didn't turn out exactly like you had hoped, you still achieved a tremendous amount and you should be proud of yourself.

For other individuals, the issue is that they often settle for anything less if their goal doesn't come true the first time they attempt it. A decent experience is worth its weight in gold, so this may not be a terrible thing. However, a wonderful experience is priceless. Furthermore, if you don't at least try for the brass ring, you'll always wonder how different life would have been if you had. So don't give up and don't settle.

www.ingramcontent.com/pod-product-compliance
Lightning Source LLC
Chambersburg PA
CBHW061425160726
47995CB00003B/760